43

Yasonda Ford

Presentation by *BookLeaf Publishing*

Web: www.bookleafpub.com

E-mail: info@bookleafpub.com

ISBN: 9789357613927

First edition 2022

*For my baby birds: Destiny, Dylan,
Dawson, & Daniya*

Agony

it's the noise of silence that triggers it

while the faithful moon shines in all its glory

loneliness reigns

wine can't drown this itch

pills dissolve in weary tears of what was once
comfort

fairytale dreams are stained with confusion
and loss

sandwiched between conviction and flesh yet the
heart endures

synchronized to scattered thoughts as night
proceeds to chase

the pangs of longing knock intensely on desire's
window

giving way to a dark place

the grief binds elevation

almost unbearable
honor's vacant seat leaves the soul restless

emptiness thrives in the night

it guts the spirit

leaving dread and fatigue to pick up its pieces by
dawn

night is cruel to the heartbroken

hour by hour relentlessly co-signing fear and
unworthiness

the darkness is eager to ridicule

slow to motivate

and abundant in shame

so we optimistically wait

while we cry

while we pray

for the morning

The Gift

Because He Lives
The deepest part of my soul searches for Him
His presence enables me to be
I'm no longer enslaved to conformity
Resurrected thoughts to resurrected minds
I'm free
In defiance I began
Abused and treasured by carnal love
My temple defaced with the graffiti of
ignorance, lust, and pain
But God had a plan
His Son was made to defend me
His life ransomed for mine, as I continue to be
reborn
My internal thoughts are drowning the external
flesh that once led me
Satan is now recognizable
No longer camouflaged by things that
Look good
Feel good
Or sound good
Tears that tainted Mary's face on Calvary aren't
in vain
Her mourning turned to morning glory
The tomb is triumphantly empty

We're released from all the things we thought we
knew
And all the things we thought we were
Engulfed by flames of grace
Consumed by the smoke of the righteous
We're all one
Seekers and thinkers
Givers and worshippers
Connected by the same blood
Because He lives

A Walking Time Bomb

How much weight can a nigga take
Knowing that his life can be taken by the
decisions he makes

The pressures of knowing he can be killed at any
moment
Being pulled over because of the color of his
skin, taking nonstop torment

He sees the homies drop like flies in a horrid
state of gang violence
The entire hood knows what's happening but
there still remains a silence

Or it just might be the stress of teenage
fatherhood
How's a fatherless man supposed to be one will
never be understood

But instead of dealing with these pressures in
another way
The evil pushes him to make someone else's life
grey

Now all these attacks are starting to unfold

And just like a walking time bomb he begins to
explode

Try spending your life dodging and ducking,
hurting and crying
beaten and humiliated while folks keep lying

Being treated inhumane is no longer apart of the
plan
How long do you think you can keep hitting a
man

Faith

There is something that surrounds our talk and
cushions every step of our daily walks and
focuses our thoughts on things unseen
It transforms our persona into the adorning tears
that tainted Mary's face on calvary
It's the reason we witness without fail and
confess without delay
We believe and we stand on it
We eat, drink, bathe, and sleep on it
It's the reason we say goodbye and I'll see you
tomorrow
It's why we plan ahead and why we rely on
God's word to keep us headed in the right
direction
It's the way we respond to the gospel and how
we manage to collect ourselves and praise him
in the middle of the storm, trials, and tribulations
that life may bring
This it, is the key that opens the door to our
inheritance of everlasting life and promise
We embrace it
Mountains of grace abide in it
Our lives our based on it
While our dreams derived from it
We lavishly worship in it

While His praise is brought fourth through it
God's approval is gained through it, and with
just enough to measure a mustard seed it assures
our salvation
What is this it?
It is faith.

Table for Two

To my dear and faithful love
I saw you hurt today,
I watched you hang your head, and shed some
tears in such a sorrowful way.

I was behind you in the grocery store
as you thought about my favorite dish,
Being with you in the flesh is all that I could
wish.

I smiled at you through the baby you held at
church today,
you felt me with the cool breeze as you walked
outside the other day.

I protected you in the car as you rode down the
street,
I sang to you within the lyrics on the radio, you
never missed a beat.

I hugged you through your pajamas you put on
to go to bed,
and I kissed you though the pillow in which you
laid your head.

Close your eyes my love and always remember
this to be true,
I love you more than life itself, there was no me
without you.

Faith is our reservation for a seat in Heavens's
blue,
and I'll be right here waiting with dinner and a
table for two.

Mahogany Woman

I was once an African Queen
In lands as far as you can see
Until one day they stole my nobility

I then became a slave
shackles, pains, and chains
losing my identity
taking on a foreign name

being raped and beaten
i continued to pray
because i knew my God would free us someday

strong is my body, strong in my mind
my days of weakness are fer left behind

I have a face of survival
eyes like ebony marbles
and skin like mahogany

Arise My Love

Arise my love and kiss me in the morning dew,
not a care in the world because it's just us two.

Arise my love because you make my heart sing,
and for your love I'll give everything.

With hope in us a future is what's in store,
so arise my love and give me love forever more.

Free Dancer

When I dance I'm a little girl again

Naive yet smarter than my age allows me to be

I'm full of play, cotton candy and sweet thangz

I close my eyes and leap over mountains

Twirl through stars

and hopscotch through rain

When I dance I'm a teenager

I know everything there is to know

and as long as I have my tap shoes

I'm free

I'm in a world of

giggles

blue jeans

and boys

When I dance I'm a lady

I've overcome obstacles and goals

yet still takes time to smell the roses

I'm full of pride

love

jasmine and lavender

When I dance I feel peace

I feel the rhythm

I feel God

Friendship

Friendship is something that you can not
measure,
it's organic, a gift, a unique treasure.

Communication, trust, honesty, and caring,
are all responsibilities of a lifetime of sharing.

Having a loving relationship and spending time
together,
creating very special memories that can make a
friendship last forever.

Adore You

No one can measure my endless endearment for
you
the passion in your eyes, sentiment in your
touch, the little things you do

Tranquility in your caress, aspiration in your
embrace
having a strong desire, longing to see the
loveliness of your face

My heart is full of joy whenever I'm with you
my soul is cared for and dreams no longer blue

Incessant adoration is what I have to give
a lifetime of peaceful love for as long as I live

All About Me

You've criticized the way I speak, think, and act
talked about my kinky hair and asked why my
skin is so black

Constantly you've dogged me and stepped all on
feet
told me what to do and when I didn't corporate, I
got beat

It's taken years of struggle and strife but now
you finally see
that the pain you gave doesn't hurt anymore, and
now it's all about me

I'm gorgeous, from these flat feet all the way to
these big lips
I move proudly with my wide nose and curves in
these hips

African royalty rolled up into luscious
chocolate...sweet caramel...legs that stretch a
mile and the whole room lights up when I smile

Intelligence on 10, we've came, saw, and
conquered

shattered glass ceilings your thoughts, we can't
be bothered

We were the royalty of Africa and we still
maintain our clout
truthful in our say and spiritual wisdom that
departs our mouths

You see through blinders that objectify, one day
you'll ultimately see
how the world doesn't revolve around your
hatred and now it's all about me

Driving Blind

Tears beating hard on my soul like rain on my
windshield,
 blurring my vision and distorting my view
because of my broken wiper.
How long can I drive like this?
Out of control?
Over the limit?
Nothing but roadblocks ahead of me ready to
reject my passage.
The drops are getting louder, first I see green.
Then I see red.
Yielding to my heartache.
Breaking to my sorrow.
One mile to the next exit and I wonder if I
should take it.
The town is called Heaven and my current path
is called Hell.
As I approach a rest stop, I headed straight for
the garbage can.
I threw away,
promiscuity
fear
and
loneliness.
I bought me some courage,

some peace
some hope
and life from the vendor.
I stocked up on
joy
forgiveness
holiness
and love.
I strapped on my seat belt and protected myself
with the Word.
I drove towards the exit and the tears stopped
briefly.
I couldn't hear pain on the radio anymore.
When I pulled into the town there was a young
girl walking towards me.
With the words angel on her shirt, she smiled at
me while pointing right and said Heaven is your
Destiny.
I watched her skip across the road as her dark
curls blew in the breeze.
I noticed the road change.
The sun was out now.
For once I could see clearly.
I made it.

First Love

Passionate kisses to a love that's brand new,
promise to stay with me forever because I'll die
without you.

I'm in love and it shows in everything I do,
please don't ever leave, there's no me with you.

Unconditional love to my heart is the injection,
care and consistency with no room for rejection.

My love for you the world can never take from
me,
I'll die without you love, absolutely.

Programming

we watch
we be
we cook
we see
Just what they want us all to be
we flip
we rage
we talk
we daze
into the latest media craze
we seek
we find
we laugh
we dine
at others expense both yours and mine
we argue
we take
we agree
we shake
we live
we learn
we hear
3rd degree burns
The media only perpetuates
stereotypes and accentuates

the ugly
the bad
and the worst of us
It's enough to make you scream or cuss
we tune in
we surf
we click
we hit
we copy
we paste
we print that shit
we run
we tell
we repeat
we run
we tell
we repeat
we run
we tell
we repeat
WE RUN. WE TELL. WE REPEAT.

From The Moment I Saw You

As the thermometer reaches 88 degrees
I gently allow the tawny water rise above my
knees
As I wade and splash I didn't have a clue
how my life would be when I depart this faded
blue
Turning to my right I saw the silhouette of a man
all through my body curious chills ran
With water droplets flowing from his mocha
chest
I fixed my eyes on his smile
and on his smile they would rest
With the sun's rays bouncing off his mahogany
skin
I could feel a divine attraction coming from
within
Eyes like coffee gems
they seem to reflect a light
and it was then at that moment I knew it was
love at first sight
Warm sand under our feet as we walked along
the shoreline
I still can't believe this beautiful person could be
mine

Sent straight from heaven he's my gift from God
I know love at first sight to most seems odd
But this person, in him is where my heart resides
and I'll always love him until the deepest sea
goes dry

Anticipating Your Arrival

I can feel every move you make, I feel your
breath on me,
I flinch with every step you take, through my
eyes are how you see.

You are so near yet so far, I can tell you are in
this place
The suspense is killing me, when will you show
your face?

Everywhere I go you're always there, both
directions left & right,
constantly on my mind first in the morning and
last at night.

We share the same soul, your heart beats
because of mine,
I haven't even met you yet it feels like a lifetime.

My health and strength are the keys to your
survival,
you feed off me and take from me to complete
your arrival.

When I look into the mirror I see a different
face,
my body is distorted and has taken on a new
shape.

I wonder if you'll like me, or be impressed with
me at all,
I think about your features or if you will be short
or tall.

It's almost time for us to meet and I still don't
have a clue, on how to speak, think or act, or
even take care of you.

I've been counting down the days and I have a
little while,
to become a brand new mother and meet my first
born child.

All I know is that I need you and I pray to God
you'll be okay,
when I finally get to hold you on that night or
winter day.

FYI

through wide nostrils passes inherited air that
fills the lungs of cocoa queens giving oxygen to
hands that deliver babies
legs that walk the walk
and tongues that preach power
my womb creates wombs
behind these black frames is a black frame
disguised behind the stereotype that goes with
my unconventional name
I embody the mother's that walked before me
my inhale is the exhale of grace
not a punching bag for sore egos and past hurt
I'm not your catch all
If something is wrong with you
I did it
If something didn't work for you
I broke it
If I lead I'm aggressive
If I follow I'm too submissive
Angry Black females weren't born they were
created

Deliverance

The deepest part of my soul is searching for
Him.

To be in His presence enables me.

I'm no longer enslaved to conformity.

I'm free to explore the benefits of my faith which
are blessings.

I began defiant.

I abused the unconditional love of Christ and
treasured the carnal love of the world.

What was supposed to be my temple was
nothing more than an abandoned play ground
defaced with the grafitti of ignorance, lust, pain,
and shame.

But God had a plan.

Then as new as the morning Sun He paraded my
sins with forgiveness.

This gift was always there for me.

The rebirth of my spirit and transformation has
given me life.

A life that mirrors those who walked before me.

My internal thoughts are drowning the external
flesh that once lead me.

Evil is now recognizable.

No longer camouflaged by things that look
good, feel good, or sound good.

I'm more than what my flesh allowed me to be.

I'm that which God says I'am.

The beauty is God and His love for me.

The chains are gone.

The shackles released.

The curses are broken.

It's deliverance.

#2

When I first heard you were coming, I wanted to
pack up and leave town, or lock my doors and
turn off the lights to pretend no one was around.

Your soon to be presence intimidated me, and I
felt incredibly weak.
I cried silent tears and of your arrival I did not
speak.

Being unprepared and somewhat ashamed I
wondered what others thought of me, did they
see my obvious confusion or lack of
responsibility.

As months passed by my feelings changed and I
learned I was having a son,
I then began to face my fears because my new
life has just begun.

Fast forward to today and I appreciate the
blessings given to me, to have not one but many
children who love me unconditionally.